Seven Keys
Economic Empowerment

© 2000 Phillip Phinn
Published by Phillip S. Phinn
E-mail: phillipphinn@gmail.com
ISBN#: 978-1-365-72452-7
Revised 2020, 2023

All scripture quotations unless noted otherwise arc from the Holy Bible, King James version.

Take note that the name Satan and related named arc not capitalized. We choose not to acknowledge him, even to the point of violating grammatical rules.

Table of Contents

Preface 3

Acknowledgments 5

CHAPTER 1 - The Mustard Seed Model 6

CHAPTER 2 - How To Earn Multiple Income 13

CHAPTER 3 - Divine Guidance - The Number One Key To

Prosperity 20

CHAPTER 4 - An Alternative Approach to Welfarism 26

CHAPTER 5 - Discoveries and Development............................ 33

CHAPTER 6 - Every Man is a Businessman 39

CHAPTER 7 - Principles of the Mustard Seed Model 47

CHAPTER 8 - Key Principles - The Principle of Work.............. 54

CHAPTER 9 The Path of No Return.. 64

About The Author.. 73

Preface

Daily our news media are filled with such gruesome stories of starvation, famine, foreclosures, bankruptcies, layoffs, recession, poverty, unemployment, and civil wars.

Men's hearts are failing them for fear of all these things. Experts, economists, social scientists, and politicians are perplexed and "stressed-, out" as they see only a gloomy future. Why is there cause for concern when there is no lack or scarcity of material and human resources on planet earth?

Organization of Petroleum Exporting Countries (OPEC) has to be begging members to cut back on their quotas so as to avoid a glut on the world market. Farmers in the USA have been given incentives to cut back on production as well.

Are you aware that only a fraction of the earth's rich deposits has been tapped, coupled with the tremendous human potential that is locked up in approximately six billion people on planet earth? You may therefore be asking, why is there so much human need and suffering? The answer my friend, is no longer *"blowing in the wind"*. Certainly, poverty and most of the ills that face mankind are caused by man's lust, greed, selfishness, and wickedness; ills oftentimes motivated by the love of money. The apostle Paul was right when he said, *"The love of money is the root of all evil."* (Take careful note of this) He did not say, *"Money is the root of all evil."*

I am convinced that every person is born with at least one innate gift, that given the opportunity to develop, poverty and unemployment would be avoided; in fact, the sky would be the limit with respect to their prosperity and achievements.

Lee Kwan Yew, ex-prime minister of Singapore, says: *"A Singaporean's ability to rise depends upon his innate gifts and his application."*

The principle of the mustard seed is one that we have been applying since 1986, which started first in my own local church and now in many nations of the world. Wherever people have applied this principle the results have always led to substantial financial and economic breakthrough.

Acknowledgments

I wish to thank my editor for coordinating the production and publishing of this book.

Also, I must make special mention of Araya Crosskill for his editorial assistance and Joy Humphrey for typing this manuscript at short notice.

I am especially grateful to the late Dr. Myles Munroe, my apostolic counsellor for encouraging me to write. The prophetic words received from Dr. Ken Roberts, Dr. Leslie Rogers, Joan Thomas, and Debbie Russell spurred me on to obey God to write this book.

Thanks be to God.

CHAPTER 1 - The Mustard Seed Model

The mustard seed model is based on the principles of:

- Vision and Purpose - Proverbs 29:18
- Small Beginnings - Zechariah 4; 10; Job 8:7; Matthew 13: 31-32
- Work - Proverbs 22:29
- Investment - Luke 19:12
- Perseverance - Luke 18: 1-8
- Faith - Mark: 23-24; Proverbs 23:7 (Focus Faith)
- Goal setting - Luke 14: 28-32

It is written in the Bible, *"Despite not the days of small beginnings."* It is also written, *"The kingdom of heaven is like a grain of mustard seed, which a man took, and sowed in his field, which indeed is the least of all seeds, but when it is grown, it is the greatest among herbs, and becometh a tree, so that the birds of the air come and lodge in the branches thereof."*

The poorest man is a man without a vision. Once you can determine where you would like to go, the first step is to begin. Begin with what you have. With hard work and determination, you will be able to fulfil your dream.

The Mustard Seed Principle seeks to give everyone a chance to fulfil his or her dream. The traditional method of acquiring capital to start a business is by way of a bank loan. However, in order to qualify for a loan, one has got to have collateral or get someone who has collaterals to stand security for the loan. Many dreams fail to materialize as dreamers waited in vain to acquire the starting capital to launch out into their enterprise.

The Mustard Seed Principle says. START WITH WHAT YOU HAVE. Don't wait, move ahead like Jack.

The Story of Jack[1]

Jack's dream was to own and operate his own supermarket. He grew up in poverty. As a result, he did not do well in school, and as a grown young man was barely making ends meet. Nevertheless, he had a dream and was determined to see the fulfilment of his dream.

He started off by selling newspapers and then from the profit he added hot dogs, bread and cheese and soft drinks. It was not long before he established his own grocery shop. His grocery shop eventually grew into a supermarket. Jack, however, did not stop at the supermarket. He went on to own a chicken farm, a bakery, a garage, and an insurance agency.

---

[1] *Jack was used to avoid calling names - and is the stunning story of interviews and discussion with several stories - From Rags to Riches.*

My Own Story

After discovering this principle thirteen years ago, I decided to put it to work in my life first before I started to teach it to others. In 1986 I started with eight hundred (J$800) dollars, selling books and audiocassettes. At the end of the first year I turned the eight hundred (J$800) dollars into eighteen thousand (J$18,000) dollars.

Now a seed of eighteen thousand (J$18,000) dollars can do much more than J$800. I used J$7,000 to establish an acre of coffee, J$3,000 to plant an acre of cocoa, and J$2,000 to start a school supply business (selling pens, rubbers, exercise books etc.). By 1989 I had enough to publish my first book, *"How to be a World Overcomer."* By 1991 I had three books published. My dream as a businessman and a self-publisher is being fulfilled without having to borrow one cent.

Zorima's Story

In the book *"Give Us Credit"* by Alex Courts (Pages. 46-47) the Zorima story is proof that the Mustard Seed Principle is a major key for the eradication of poverty. Zorima Begum, a beggar woman who was three times married was thrice deserted by her husbands, came to know about the bank loan (i.e., the Grameen Bank in Bangladesh that gave loans without collateral).

Overcoming her fears, she took a loan of 250 taka (US$6.00). She invested the money in trading grocery goods in the neighborhood. She paid off the entire loan in weekly instalments. She did not have any problem. As soon as the first loan was repaid, she took a second loan. This time she was bold. She borrowed 1000 taka (US$25.00).

Now she is an independent businesswoman.

Mohammed Suleman's Story

I was in Britain on the 16 May 1999 and happened to pick up the Sunday Mirror, and saw the following headline, *"Tycoons with a Heart!"* Mr. Suleman and his son, who is also a millionaire, were handing out more than £10,000 in £50 notes to a group of startled Kosovan refugees. Mohammed was a refugee when India was partitioned in 1947. He went to Pakistan and from there to England. He arrived in Huddlesfield, West Yorkshire, in 1962.

With only £25 in his pocket, he got a job as a coalman and after two years he had saved enough to start a small Asian food store. He prospered and developed that small store into a chain of stores. He moved north to Glasgow in 1971 and opened a number of corner shops.

In 1976 the business expanded into clothing outlets. Soon he and his son had made enough to start a large cash-and-carry warehouse selling electrical goods and kitchen equipment to the catering trade. More than 50 people now work for the father and son in a warehouse located on five and a half acres of land in Glasgow. When Mr. Suleman and his son heard that a group of refugees were being housed in Glasgow Tower block they were determined to help.

Mohammed said that he knew what it was like to have nothing and to be dispossessed of everything. His son also said that they have worked very hard for what they had, but everyone needs a helping hand, and he suggested that the money could be used to help one or two persons to start a business.

Undoubtedly, there have been many refugees who migrated to England from India and Pakistan with Mr. Suleman who are still struggling in jobs trying to make ends meet. What is the difference between Mr. Suleman and the other refugees - *luck?* I don't think so.

I submit to you that this man, like numerous persons in various success cases that I have read and examined over the years, applied these seven principles:

> 1. He had a burning vision - a purposeful vision to become an independent business owner.
> 2. He started small - a humble beginning with one small Asian food store.
> 3. He worked very hard and smart.

4. He invested and reinvested his money and from one small store developed a chain of stores.

5. He triumphed over his business challenges by applying the principle of perseverance.

6. He believed in his vision/dream. He believed that he could accomplish what he set out to do - he exercised the principle of faith.

7. He expanded step by step. He set himself various goals and worked towards them.

If all the other refugees had similar dreams/visions like Mr. Suleman, they too would have been equally successful. Notwithstanding, ninety- seven per cent of the world's population is financially illiterate and most of us have been socialized to think of working for money all the days of our lives; meanwhile the remaining three per cent who control most of the world's resources have been trained to have money work for them.

The primary purpose of this book is to enlighten my third world brothers and sisters regarding the truth about economic empowerment. I broke the poverty cycle in my life with US$150. Since then, I have been sharing these principles with thousands of people around the world. You too can do the same.

Notes

Key Points

_____

_____

_____

_____

_____

_____

Personal Thoughts

_____

_____

_____

_____

Areas for additional research

_____

_____

_____

_____

CHAPTER 2 - How To Earn Multiple Income

A few years ago, I was preparing for a financial seminar when I was led 10 this portion of scripture in II Kings 4: 1-7 (KJV):

"Now there cried a certain woman of the wives of the sons of the prophets unto Elisha, saying, Thy servant my husband is dead; and thou knowest that thy servant did fear the Lord: and the creditor is come to take unto him my two sons to be bondmen.

And Elisha said unto her, what shall I do for thee? Tell me, what hast thou in the house? And she said, thine handmaid hath not anything in the house, save a pot of oil.

Then he said, Go, borrow thee vessels abroad of all thy neighbors, even empty vessels, and thou shalt set aside that which is full.

And when thou art come in, thou shalt shut the door upon thee and upon thy sons, and shalt pour out into all those vessels, and thou shalt set aside that which is full.

So, she went from him, and shut the door upon her and upon her sons, who brought the vessels to her; and she poured out.
And it came to pass, when the vessels were full, that she said unto her son, bring me yet a vessel. And he said unto her, there is not a vessel more. And the oil stayed.

Then she came and told the man of God, and he said, Go, sell the oil, and pay thy debt, and live thou and thy children of the rest."

I had previously read this portion of scripture several times but on this particular day I heard the Lord speaking to me about vessels.

He said, *"Most of my people have only one vessel called salary."* I see clearly from this passage that God only stopped pouring the oil when the woman ran out of vessels.

It is never God's responsibility to provide us with vessels. You must provide Him with the vessels, and He will fill them.

In the book of Isaiah when God was getting ready to bless and promote His people, He told the prophet Isaiah - Isaiah 54: 2-3 KJV *"Enlarge the place of thy tent, and let them stretch for the curtains of thine habitations: spare not, lengthen thy cords, and strengthen thy stakes; For thou shall break forth on the right hand and on the left; and thy seed shall inherit the Gentiles, and make the desolate cities to be inhabited."*

Do you want God to bless you? Provide him with the rooms, the baskets, the vessels. If you give him ten baskets, he will fill all ten. Similarly, if you give him only one; he will fill only one.

If you are a preacher or pastor and praying for God to give you a church of five hundred members, and the place you have provided for God to put these five hundred only seats one hundred, then you are trying to get God to do your job for you. God's promises are conditional — there is the *'God-side'* and the *'man-side.'* God said, for example, *"If my people who are called by my name shall:*
(1)   Humble themselves;
(2)   Pray;
(3)   Turn from their wicked ways.
(4)   Seek his face;

Then he will:
(1)   Hear;
(2)   Forgive our sins;
(3)   Heal our land." 2 Chron. 7: 14 KJV.

God requested us to do four things and promised that if we did these, he would do three things.

However, how often we find folks trying to get God to do these three things without doing what he had requested. God is saying, if you desire more than one income bring more than one basket to me. You want my blessings; enlarge the place of your tent.

Since that day, I have been showing various people and professionals how to earn multiple incomes. I remember teaching along this line in Barbados and a dentist who had attended the seminar approached me and asked, *"How can I as a dentist earn more than one income apart from my dental practice?"* I interviewed him, and based on the information he gave to me, I did a *"multiple income analysis"* for him. The results were as follows:

1) Income from his practice
2) Income from trading in dental supplies
3) Income from various types of investments:
   a. Real estate
   b. Mutual fund
   c. Stocks, shares, bonds, etc.
4) Income from lecturing and consultancy

I showed him how he could invest in himself to become the leading dentist in the island and as a result he could lecture in dental schools, write books, produce tapes and open other dental offices. He saw clearly how he could maximize his potential to earn income from another nine avenues.

Multiple Incomes for a Computer Science Teacher

1) Textbooks in computer science
2) Textbooks in other languages
3) Tapes - audio and video
4) Establishing a training institute
5) Trading in computer products
6) Investments (in various areas)
7) Education - resulting in more lecturing and consulting.
8) Teacher's salary
9) Other

Earning multiple incomes means a radical departure from the traditional way of thinking. Ninety-seven percent (97%) of the world's population is socialized to think *"working for money"* and once you think working for money, you can only think of working two or more jobs for multiple income. The first thing that you have to do is think *"money working for me."*

Developing a mentality of having money work for you will get you on a path of finding ways and means to earn, invest and re-invest, eventually freeing you from living from one pay cheque to another. Freeing you to do what you were born to do, but could not do because of bills and other financial constraints. Money must become our slave and work for us, so that we can do what we were born to do. You will never know true success until you are working in the area of your God-given mission in life.

How about beginning today? Put a plan of action in place so that within the next three to five years you will have money working for you. This will free you to serve God in the ministry, in government or wherever your mission in life will take you.

In closing this chapter, I will do one final multiple income analysis for a missionary:

1) Speaking engagements
2) Income from the sale of books and tapes
3) Faith - *"give, and it shall be given unto you"* (seven times over) (St. Luke 6: 38)
4) Investments
5) Others: e.g., trading (find a need and fill it)
6) Earnings from skills, e.g., teaching, musical talents, etc.

Notes

Key Points

_____

_____

_____

_____

_____

_____

Personal Thoughts

_____

_____

_____

_____

Areas for additional research

_____

_____

_____

_____

CHAPTER 3 - Divine Guidance - The Number One Key To Prosperity

The woman in II Kings chapter 4: 1-7 got divine guidance and instructions that helped her to come out of her financial crisis.

Isaac got divine directions to stay in the land of famine, and God blessed him. Isaac sowed within a twelve-month period and received the hundredfold blessing (Genesis 26: 1-12).

The Shunammite woman received divine guidance through prophet Elisha to flee the land of famine for seven years and at the end of that period she entered into a financial harvest that made her wealthy for the rest of her life (II Kings 4: 1-6). Where God leads, he provides. Every God given vision attracts provision. The minute Mary said yes to God, the camels with provision for baby Jesus started moving towards her.

"He leadeth me beside the still waters". "He leadeth me in the paths of righteousness." Psalm 23

"Seek ye first the Kingdom of God and His righteousness and all these things shall be added unto you." Matthew 6:33

"For the Kingdom of God is not meat and drink but righteousness, and peace and joy in the Holy Ghost." Romans 14:17

". . . much more they who receive abundance of grace, and the gift of righteousness shall reign in life by One, Jesus Christ." Romans 5: 17

Genesis 26: tells us that there was a famine in the land where Isaac was, and everybody was running to Egypt where there was food and other comforts.

But *"The Lord appeared unto him (Isaac) and said, go not down into Egypt (Egypt in the scriptures is a type of the world); Dwell in the land that I shall tell thee of." "Sojourn in this land, and I will be with thee, and will bless thee, for unto thee and unto thy seed, I will perform the oath which I swore unto Abraham thy father."*

Key: Dwell in the land that, I (God) shall tell thee of. Saints, the Lord has a personal/specific plan for your life. He says: *"For we are his workmanship, created in Christ Jesus unto good works, which God hath before ordained that we should walk in them."* (Ephesians 2: 10). You have to walk in them! He is ready and willing to lead us in them.

The specific will/plan of God for your life must come to you by way of revelation *"but as it is written, eye hath not seen, nor ear heard, neither have entered into the heart of man the things which God hath prepared for them that love Him,"* (I Corinthians 2: 9). Thus, He says, *"But God hath revealed them unto us by His Spirit,"* (I Corinthians 2: 10).

God will reveal them unto us by His Spirit. Thus, it behooves us to pray for the spirit of wisdom and revelation. Paul, the apostle, prayed this prayer for the saints in Ephesians 1: 1523. He prayed specifically for three things, *"that we may know":*

(1) Purpose
The hope of His calling, that is, His Call Vocation -Will for our life.

(2) Potential
The riches of the glory of his inheritance in the Saints (His inheritance for you).

(3) Power
The exceeding greatness of His resurrection power that is available to you as a believer.

God wants us to know so that we will not be destroyed for lack of knowledge. *"We have received the Spirit of God that we might know the things that are freely given to us of God."* (I Corinthians 2: 12).

Remember! — "Dwell in the land that I shall tell thee of." "And Isaac dwelt in Gerar" **(Genesis 26:6).**

"Then Isaac sowed in that land and received in the same year at hundredfold — and the Lord blessed Him," (Genesis 26: 12).

Will you allow the Lord to lead you this year into that land? If you are already in that land, then sow faithfully, the hundredfold is yours this year.

Then Peter began to say unto Him, lo we have left all, and have followed Thee. And Jesus answered and said, *" Verily I say unto you, there is no man that hath left houses, or brethren, or sisters, or father or mother, or wife or children or lands for my sake and the Gospel's but he shall receive an hundredfold, now in this time"* (Mark 10: 28— 30).

Now is the time — this year!

Notes on Divine Guidance

Some steps to be taken to receive a specific word from the Lord:

(1) Be neutral — not your Will — His Will.

(2) Pray for 1 His Divine Desire - Psalm 37: 4, Proverbs 10: 24, Mark 11: 24.

(3) Scriptural agreement: that is, what you perceive to be His Divine Desire for your life must be in agreement with the scripture. The

Lord will not lead you to invest in the illegal drug trade.

(4)Look for an open door.

(5)Discern His timing (key to this is His Supernatural Peace).

The 4 "IONS"
(Practice the principle of the 4 "IONS"):

(1)Meditation

Meditate upon guidance scriptures: Get your mind renewed with them - Psalm 32:8, Psalm 16:11, Romans 8:14, Proverbs 3:5-6, Psalm 23:1, Isaiah 58:11, I Corinthians 2:12.

(2)Confession

Always confess guidance scriptures. You will have what you say - Mark 11:23.

(3)Intercession

Pray with these scriptures as you claim God's promises. Pray in tongues as well as in English (Romans 8: 26-27). The Holy Spirit knows how to pray God's perfect will for you.

(4)Action

Act upon what the Holy Spirit reveals to you. *"And the peace of God, which passeth all understanding shall keep your hearts and mind through Christ Jesus"* - (Philippians 4: 7).

Notes

Key Points

_____

_____

_____

_____

_____

Personal Thoughts

_____

_____

_____

Areas for additional research

_____

_____

_____

_____

CHAPTER 4 - An Alternative Approach to Welfarism

We discovered that it is usually the unskilled that are poor and unemployed. There is an old Chinese proverb that says, *"Give a hungry man a fish today and he will he hungry again tomorrow, but teach him to fish and he will never he hungry again."*

In our approach to helping the poor and the unemployed, we have always sought to find out what they can do and want to do. We would help train the untrained, and to those that are skilled we make available interest-free loans. Traditional welfarism has robbed people of their self-worth and often exploited their labour.

In 1986 I met a young man, 18 years old, who was getting J$40.00 per week from his church. I knew that their intention was pure, but in reality, they were doing more harm than good to this young man. I stopped the payment immediately and then asked the young man to go home and write a letter stating what he wanted in life. In his letter he outlined that he believed that he had a gift in fashion designing, and would like to pursue a career in this field.

I worked along with a businessman in the church to get this young man in the government garment manufacturing school. The school gave him a little money while he learned. A year later he graduated with a skill, and today he is producing and selling his product not just locally but internationally.

They would have destroyed this young man's future if they had continued to give him the forty dollars (J$40.00) each week. I believe even the cripple and the blind can be trained and helped to make an honest living for themselves.

The Two-Fold Purpose of Money

Money that we can earn should be used basically for two purposes:

> (1) Provide bread to eat,
> (2) Provide seed to sow.

If one, however, eat; everything he earns, he is sure to remain poor. In order to overcome poverty, we must not only work for money, but we must let money work for us. We must therefore set aside "X" amount of money for investment.

We have advised those using the Mustard Seed Principle to make great sacrifice in the first three years in order to have capital to plough back into their business, thus ensuring continuous growth and expansion.

Many of our members who ran their business on the side were able to switch from their place of employment, pay themselves a salary, take care of their overhead expenses and still have profit left over to plough back into their business for expansion and growth.

Testimonials

Aglow Fashions

In 1986 I started selling ice-pops at 50c each. However, in 1987, having been taught the Mustard Seed Principle, I used the profit of J$1,200 from selling the ice-pops as a deposit on an industrial sewing machine priced at J$7,000. This machine was paid for in three (3) months from the sale of garments made. Another machine, (a serger), was purchased for J$8,000. This was also paid for in three (3) months.

A second industrial machine, (second hand) was purchased for J$6,800 and a domestic machine for J$3,000. This was being done at home while I held a full-time job. In June 1988 I resigned my job, moved the business from home and rented a shop for J$1,200 monthly.

In 1989 as a result of problems with staff, I was forced to give up the shop and move the business back home to save it from total collapse. All the funds were now depleted, and I had to take another job. From home, the business was gradually rebuilt; the Lord provided an excellent and honest worker who managed it in my absence. In 1990 I received many orders from a co-worker who lilted my own clothes. These were delivered promptly.

In 1991 I again began to realize a profit. Between 1991/93 the business expanded rapidly. A non-withdrawal account was opened; some of the profit was used to help needy children and to assist two other individuals to start their own business. Tithing was always done. It has been six (6) years later and the business is now operating successfully. Cash in bank and assets total J$105,000.

King's Kid Nursery

In November 1987 we began trading informally. The initial capital investment was J$7,200. This purchased US 1,000 and two (2) tickets in Miami and back. At the end of the second trip, we had J$17,700 in the bank (profit J$10,500). This was re-invested. At the end to the fourth trip, we had purchased a refrigerator, a stove and deposited J$4,400 on furniture for our next venture - a day care centre and nursery.

We suffered a setback as the stove and refrigerator were stolen in November 1990. Nevertheless, in January 1991 the doors of the Nursery we opened with three (3) children and a weekly income of J$350. At the end of that year there were twenty-five (25) children and a week income of J$3,250.

At the end of 1992 we had forty (40) children and a weekly income of J$8,000. Presently we have forty-five (45) children and a weekly income of J$13,500.

There is now J$30,000 in the bank and an asset base of approximate J$100,000.

Three points need to be noted here:
> (1) Tithing was systematically done.
> (2) The Mustard Seed Principle was practiced.
> (3) The nursery operates debt free.

The Clarion Call

The clarion call in this hour is for another Industrial Revolution. The revolution must emerge from the Third World. In fact, the reason why we are called *"Third World"* is mainly because we did not benefit from the first Industrial Revolution.

As we continue to inspire our people and help them to discover their innate gifts and to become creative, many marvelous discoveries will take place.

Dr. George Washington Carver created a revolution for southern agriculture and industry in the USA when he discovered over three hundred products from the peanut. I am convinced that there are thousands of industries and products in the foods, plants, miner and other natural resources waiting to be discovered in Third World nations.

Over the last decade we have begun to see a little breakthrough here mil there. For example, two doctors in

Jamaica discovered the cure for glaucoma from the marijuana plant. They produced a drug called *"Canasol"*.

Another local company made a drink derived from the grapefruit. The drink is called *"Ting"*. Ting brought in millions of dollars in foreign exchange. It won four gold medals in Luxemburg 1977; Geneva 1978; Paris 1979 and Amsterdam in 1992.

The Aloe Vera plant, which grows wild in the Third World, is a source of many products. It staggers the mind.

Garlic is another plant from which many products are being derived. I am persuaded that there are more products and industries in garlic than Carver found in the peanut.

We should also take note of what the Israelites did with the barren, desert land that they were given. They have become totally self-sufficient in food and are the world's largest suppliers of flowers.

Let us not forget too, the potential that we have in the field of music, sports, the arts and technical skills. There is much talk today about recovery and growth in our economics. I tell you, indeed there is no recovery and growth except that which will come through DISCOVERIES.

Notes

Key Points

_____

_____

_____

_____

_____

Personal Thoughts

_____

_____

_____

_____

Areas for additional research

_____

_____

_____

_____

CHAPTER 5 - Discoveries and Development

The key to recovery and development is intercession for revival. The Holy Scripture teaches, and it is proven in history, that when God's people turn to Him in humility, confess their sins and pray for mercy and forgiveness, God promises to hear their cry and forgives their sins; sending revival, which heals the land and brings genuine prosperity.

The Wesleyan Revival

No revival occurring in the last two hundred and fifty years, serves to show us more forcefully what happens when God heals a nation, than the Wesleyan Revival. More have probably been written about this revival than all the others that have occurred. The lessons have provided much inspiration to Christians of every generation since the death of John Wesley.

John Wesley pioneered a movement of prayer in response to the moral, social, and political decline, which had swept early 18th century British society. The revival which followed dramatically reversed the decadence and ushered in unprecedented prosperity from which all Western nations derived their great wealth. The lessons of this revival are very relevant today. The revival changed 18th century Great Britain, setting her on a path of social and economic progress that caused her to dominate world politics and economics for the next two centuries.

Knate Krupp in his book The Church Triumphant described the conditions of Great Britain in the early 18th century as follows:

"Great, Britain was in desperate need; immorality, inhuman treatment of children (three out of four died before their fifth birthday), drunkenness, poverty filth, illiteracy and unbelief in God were all rampant."

The threat of bloodshed and revolution, which characterized the European continent hung like a blanket over Britain. It is interesting to note that the church was also at a very poor ebb spiritually. How did the situation change? It was changed by united concerted prayer, which was started by a small group of Christians, including John and Charles Wesley who met each evening at Oxford University between six and nine in the evenings for bible study and prayer.

By 1739 John Wesley and George Whitfield began to preach to open air crowds as large as twenty thousand and over the next forty years mighty revival came to Great Britain. Scholars who studied the Wesleyan Revival concluded that this revival not only changed the moral climate of Great Britain, but resulted also in the social and economic advancement of the nation.

Genuine national prosperity followed the Wesleyan Revival. It was called the Industrial Revolution. Max Weber the distinguished father of sociology traces the development of the Industrial Revolution from which western economic power evolved, to the Wesleyan Revival.

The Spirit of Wisdom and Revelation

Many of us have prayed earnestly for God to heal our land or nation. Have you ever stopped to think how God heals a nation, or have you made yourself available for God to use you as part of the answer?
Billions of dollars are before our eyes, but unless God opens our eyes we just cannot see.

There are things yet to be invented that can provide millions of dollars for nations, but without the spirit of wisdom and revelation at work we will remain in darkness and poverty. God showed George Washington Carver over three hundred products and industries from peanut. Carver's discoveries revolutionized agriculture and industry in the southern United States with the revelation God gave him.

There is a front-page headline in the Jamaican *Daily Gleaner* of Thursday, 10th February 1994 that serves to strengthen my arguments on how discovery is indeed the key to the recovery and growth of Third World countries. It is our time for another revolution.

The headline reads *"Breakthrough in   Treatment   of Termites."* A local scientist had made a scientific breakthrough in the treatment of termites that could not only earn foreign exchange for the country, but also cut the big import bill for environmentally unfriendly insecticides.

That scientist was Dr. Ajar Mansingh, Reader of Entomology at the University of the West Indies (UWI) Mona campus. Dr. Mansingh made the breakthrough after trying about fifteen different combinations of boric acid and various plant extracts in nearly ten years of research and two years of intensive testing.

The article went on to say: *"Jamaica's import bill for pesticides is far more than US$7 million per year and insecticides account for about US$2 million of that bill. The locally marketed product will not only cut the bill, but is projected to earn an additional US$5 million if marketed regionally."*

We need to have thousands more breakthroughs in various areas. Why should we in the Third World think or wait for Europe or America to make discoveries for the betterment of mankind? We too have been given creative minds and abilities by our Creator.

I am pleased to see and hear about technological breakthroughs coming from the Third World nations. Another scientist here in Jamaica a few years ago found the cure for glaucoma. This same scientist is now working on two Jamaican herbs to find the cure for diabetes.

Recently there was a headline in the Jamaican *Daily Gleaner* that reads: *"Diabetes Research Making Progress."* Professor Manley West, who made international news with his discovery of *"Canasol"* which treats the eye disease glaucoma, is on the search for a cure or treatment for diabetes a prevalent disease.

"Progress is being made" he told Don Cunningham, assistant general manager of marketing at the National Commercial Bank (NCB), as was presented with an annual research grant from NCB for US$20,000 Plants are being investigated, said Professor West *"... and an even more dramatic finding is that laboratory animals used in the investigation and in which diabetes had been induced, have reverted to normal when injected with the drug."*

Can you imagine the economic success that a discovery of the cure of diabetes will mean for Jamaica? I am somehow convinced it is going to happen. Over sixty million people worldwide presently have diabetes. According to a recent World Health Organization (WHO) report, they are predicting that by this year 2000, over one hundred million people on planet earth will have diabetes.

Nevertheless, we should not become complacent and wait on a few scientists to make occasional breakthroughs. There are millions of things to be invented and discovered for the advancement and development of our world. Pray and find out what part you should play so that you too can be numbered among world changers.

Notes

Key Points

_____

_____

_____

_____

Personal Thoughts

_____

_____

_____

_____

Areas for additional research

_____

_____

_____

_____

_____

CHAPTER 6 - Every Man is a Businessman

Every man is a businessman! Every woman is a businesswoman! We have been socialized to believe that business is only for a privileged few. Still, there are some of us who want to go into business while others are looking for a business opportunity or a good business deal. I have good news for you - God has ordained that you be a successful entrepreneur.

Proverbs 18: 16 says, *"A man's gift maketh room for him, and bringeth him before great men."* This gift, (man's gift), must not be confused with the gift of Christ (Roman 6: 23), the gift of the Holy Spirit (Acts 2: 38) and the gifts of the Holy Spirit (1 Corinthians 12). Man's gift is your innate gift that God placed inside of you to bless, prosper, and promote you. This gift is to become your business.

Proverbs 22: 29 say, *"Seest thou a man diligent in his business? He shall stand before kings"* If your gift is destined to bring you before great men, and being diligent in your business is also destined to bring you before great men, (kings are great men), then we can say that your gift is your business. Note that being diligent in your, (his) business — not in someone else's business - will cause you to stand before kings. There is a unique gift that God has placed within you that if discovered and developed to its full potential is destined to take you before kings. Recall the scripture says your gift will make room for you, that is, provide opportunity for you. Secondly, it will bring you before great men — will bring promotion. This gift that I am talking about must not be confused with formal education. Formal education is not a gift.

Which university or college gave Beethoven his gift? On the other hand, some gifts will definitely require that you go through formal training in order to be certified. If God called you to become a brain surgeon, then you must go to medical school or else you will not be able to practice legally.

Discovering your gift and putting it to work will cause you to excel beyond the ordinary. I know a young man who had very little education, but he was an excellent cook. He was the personal cook for the former prime minister of Jamaica. Today, he is the personal cook for the Grecian ambassador to Ireland.

There is a gift inside of you that the world will seek you out for. Hear what the bible says to Solomon, *"And all the earth sought Solomon, to hear his wisdom which God had put in his heart."* (I King 10: 24).

The world today is suffering from a spirit of mediocrity, the chief reason being too many *"copiers"* and very few original thinkers. The legal profession is a well-paying profession, so since Jim is old enough to go to college and read for a law degree, he ends up becoming a lawyer. But what kind of a lawyer is Jim? An average one. He contributes nothing new to the profession, he is not fulfilled (although he appears to be successful), and he is only known in his little world.

The question is., was Jim born to be a lawyer? No. He was born, wired, and created to be an electronic engineer. Jim says, *"In high school I was designing and repairing television sets. I dreamed of inventing a unique television set to be used in motor cars. I was forced into this profession by my parents. They wanted me to be a lawyer, but that was just not my dream."* There are countless people in the world like Jim. They are following along, appearing to be successful, and maintaining the status quo but totally miserable and dissatisfied on the inside. Some are even contemplating suicide.

They have all abandoned their creative abilities and dreams, and by so doing they have robbed themselves of true success and fulfilment. They have also robbed the world of the development their talents would have provided. I am not impressed with a fellow who goes to the university and graduates with a degree in chemistry, gets a job as a chemist, drives a nice car and owns a nice house. To the world in general that is success and progress.

The real issue however is that this young man is just an average chemist. He is not using his gift to bring about new discoveries and development. Who knows, he could be a world class musician destined to affect millions with his music and songs. But instead, he is trapped in a chemistry laboratory in another man's company.

The scripture says, *"A man's gift maketh room for him and bringeth him before great men"* (Proverbs 18: 16). Very few are living and experiencing this promise. You can always tell when someone is functioning in their innate gift. Functioning in your innate gift will cause you to be unique. Beethoven and Mozart were musicians, but each man gives us a unique brand of music that never existed before. Your innate gift protects you from the spirit of mediocrity. *"Excellent"* and *"extraordinary"* will be among the words used to describe your contributions to planet earth.

Friends, a tremendous breakthrough is at your door. If you have not yet discovered your gift, seek the face of God today and let Him reveal your gift to you. If you know your gift, put it to work — it is your business. *"A gift is a precious stone in the eyes of him that hath it; whithersoever it turneth, it prospereth"* (Proverbs 17: 8).

It is only prudent that we heed the words of the apostle Paul. *"...study to be quiet, and to do your own business, and to work with your own hands, as we commanded you." "That ye may walk honestly towards them that are without, and that ye may have lack of nothing"* (I *Thessalonians 4: 11, 12)*. Note here that the apostle Paul is giving us the key to lack. Is there *"lack"* in your life, church, or ministry?

The key to deal with lacks is to become the head and owner of your own business. You may be asking, *"How is it possible for everyone to become the owner and head of a business? If so, who will work for us? Can we have all chiefs and no Indians?"*

Good questions. Are you aware that not every business can operate on one gift or as a sole trader? Have you ever heard of *"Neal and Massy?"* Well, Neal is not going too far without Massy. How about *"Arm and Hammer?"* Arm is not going too far without Hammer. What am I trying to tell you? Most businesses, especially medium and large, are going to require a number of gifts working together, and if you are working as an arm, and someone else as a head, and yet another as eyes, the arm must not think that he is superior to the eyes and thus try to enslave him.

Once I was teaching along this line and someone told me a story that serves to illustrate very well the concept that I want to convey to you. The person recalled going to a certain hotel and was surprised at the attitude of the workers. Even the lady making the bed did it with such grace and professionalism. She said she had to go to the manager to ascertain the reason for the work attitude of the workers being different form the usual. The manager's reply was, *"All the workers are shareholders; this hotel is owned by the workers."* That lady spreading the bed knows that she is not only spreading die bed of a hotel where she works, but she is spreading her own bed. This message is calling for two main things: (1) a redefinition of business and (2) a new economic order.

We need to re-define business. We have for too long narrowed business down to trading. So the minute a pastor, minister or a teacher hears the word *"business,"* their minds start to think — auto parts, lumber, foodstuff and so on. Are you aware that the first person to mention the word *"business"* in the New Testament was Jesus? At the age of twelve years he said, *"I must be about my Father's business."* Jesus was a businessman.

The apostle Paul writing to the Church in Rome said to them, *"Be not slothful in business"*. Every man is created, wired and ordained to work. *"For we are His workmanship, created in Christ Jesus unto good works, which God hath before ordained that we should walk in them."* (Eph. 2:10) We cannot narrow down ministry to just preaching. Who would facilitate the preacher if everybody preached? How it that there is not much emphasis on such gifts (ministries) as he that is called to show mercy, and he that is called to give. In all your travels have you ever met anyone with the gift of giving?

I have met many with the gift of *"receiving"*. Or better yet, perhaps I should ask another question, has anyone ever approached you to help pray for him to get, or stir up the gift of giving? In Romans chapter 12, the apostle Paul was addressing the issue of service through gifts given to us by God:

"Having then gifts differing according to the grace that is given to us, whether prophecy, let us prophesy according to the proportion of faith; or ministry, let us wait on our ministering; or he that teacheth, on teaching; or he that exhorteth, on exhortation; he that giveth, let him do it with simplicity; he that ruleth, with diligence; he that showeth mercy, with cheerfulness."

How spiritual is the gift of giving in this context? Notice it is placed in the context with the gift of prophecy. As the apostle continued in verse eleven (11) he said, *"Not slothful in business, fervent in spirit; serving the Lord."*

There is nothing mystical about the word *"business"* or *"businessman"*. Every man is called to be a businessman. A businessman is a man with a mission - a job and a definite purpose to fulfil. As I have been faithful to do what God has called me to do, He has always been faithful and generous in paying for his work that I get done.

Principle:

Where God leads, He provides. If God calls you to do a job and you need a ship to get that job done, He will give you a ship and that is only reasonable. None of us call in a gardener to cut the lawn and trim the hedges and expect him to do the job without tools.

Notes

Key Points

_____

_____

_____

_____

_____

_____

Personal Thoughts

_____

_____

_____

_____

Areas for additional research

_____

_____

_____

_____

CHAPTER 7 - Principles of the Mustard Seed Model

The Principle of Vision and Purpose

The poorest man is a man without a vision. Where there is no vision, people perish. Vision helps us to overcome the crippling effects of mental discouragement. Your vision empowers your life and gives you the faith and passion to go after your future focus.

Your vision must he specific and clear so that you can see yourself living in the reality of that vision. Every major event in my life was envisioned before the fulfilment of the reality.

A few years ago, I had the opportunity of hearing first-hand the Lloyd Young story. His dream was to become a body builder and win the title of Mr. Jamaica. However, he was told by his close associates that it was not possible. They said, *"You're a Chinese man with 'soft bones', therefore you are incapable of attaining your dream."*

Lloyd Young, however, refused to be discouraged. He left Montego Bay and came to Kingston to find a printer. He eventually found one and ordered one hundred and fifty stickers from him with these words in bold print - ***"LLOYD YOUNG MR. JAMAICA BODY-BUILDER."*** He returned to his home in Montego Bay and put these stickers all over his room. As he trained, he would see *"Lloyd Young Mr. Jamaica Bodybuilder."*

Seven Keys to Economic Empowerment

Everywhere he looked the vision was before him. Eight years later Lloyd Young won Mr. Jamaica body-building title and went on to represent Jamaica in a body-building competition in Kentucky, USA.

The Divine Biblical Order for the Fulfilment of your Vision

Purpose: Your vision is an assignment from God for your life.

The apostle Paul said, *"I was not disobedient to the heavenly vision."* At his conversion on the road to Damascus he asked the question, *"Lord, what will thou have me to do?"* We all need to ask this question and get an answer. The answer will become your vision/mission or purpose in life.

Paul at the end of his ministry said, *"I have finished my course . . ."* When he asked the Lord, *"What will thou have me to do?"* the Lord replied, *"Go into the city, it will be told to thee that thou must do."*

Three days later the Lord sent Ananias to affirm his call as an apostle and minister to the Gentiles, Kings, and Jews. Your vision should be so real and clear that you should be able to capture it in a phrase or a sentence.

Examples:

- Phillip Phinn - *"Teach my people how to win the battles of life."*

- Oral Roberts - *"Take my healing power to your generation."*

- Kenneth Hagin - *"Go teach my people faith."*

- Myles Munroe - *"Transforming followers into leaders."*

Preparation: The vision is for an appointed time.

Jesus spent thirty (30) years preparing for three-and one-half years of ministry.

Moses spent forty (40) years on the backside of a mountain in preparation.

Joseph spent thirteen (13) years and Paul said he spent fourteen (14) years in the Arabian Desert.

Preparation involves much prayer, study, patience, and long-suffering. (See Proverbs 13:20)

Power: Usually, after passing the test of preparation, God will release His power in you and upon you.

God appeared to Moses at the end of the 40 years of preparation in a burning bush. Luke recalled that Jesus returned to Galilee . . . *"in the power of the Spirit"* after his 40 days of fasting, trials, and testing in the wilderness. God's power working in conjunction with your potential/gift will create the next step, and that is provision. (See Proverbs 18:16).

Provision: The anointing on the life will attract people.

Your gift will make room for you and people will come and bring with them material resources. So, you now have human and material resources to support and finance your vision.

Things to do to turn your vision into reality:

(1) **Write It:** The act of writing down your vision on paper accounts for as much as fifty per cent of its fulfilment.

(2) **Be Passionate:** Anything that is not worth dying for is not worth living for. If your passion/desire/burden/motivation is not greater than the opposing circumstances that will come against your vision, it will die. If you are going to do

something great for God, you can count on facing obstacles. The greater your vision, the bigger and more frequent the obstacles you are going to face. When the going gets tough, if your heart is not in it, you will give up.

(3) **Prayer:** The purpose of prayer is to enforce and establish God's will. Jesus says, *"After this manner pray... Thy will be done..."* In our ministry, God has raised up a group of intercessors that meet weekly to pray for the fulfilment of the vision.

(4) **Focus:** If you are to achieve your vision, it is going to take a lot of concentration. It will mean denying lesser things to gain this greater vision. Too often, we find ourselves scattered in all directions. To fulfil a great vision takes singleness of mind. It has been said that what gets your attention, gets you! To fulfil a great vision, you must focus on its fulfilment.

(5) **Planning:** God has a master plan for us to enter into explosive growth in our ministries. This plan, however, must be executed in phases. You will, therefore, have to organize, delegate, and get Holy Spirit strategies every step of the way.

Success is a process. If you ever stop going for it, then you stop being successful. Success is like a staircase; one step builds upon the former step while preparing for the next step.

In summary:

(a)   You must have a dominant vision. You must have a vision that is the major purpose of your future. You must have a vision that represents what you really want.

(b)   You must see yourself already living in the reality of that vision, the vision fulfilled, visualized.

(c)   Visions must be specific. You must know exactly what you want.

Notes

Key Points

_____

_____

_____

_____

_____

_____

Personal Thoughts

_____

_____

_____

Areas for additional research

_____

_____

_____

_____

CHAPTER 8 - Key Principles - The Principle of Work

The order that we have today as it relates to ownership and employment is still one of slavery. It is far from the divine order of God whereby He created man not to be dominated by his fellowmen, but there should be a working together in mutual submission and respect.

Essentially, what we have is an educational system that says - work hard, study hard and get a good job. Such a system has done nothing more than to facilitate our transformation from chattel slavery to wage slavery. We have also been trained in our colleges and universities to manage other people's business. A new economic order is calling for more joint ownership of the means of production. A salary spells limitation. Often your salary can barely meet your basic needs.

This system causes people to see money as their chief motive for work. Our forefathers were whipped to work, and the system of slavery continues, though modified somewhat. The masses have grown accustomed to hate work, as it reminds them of the whip of the past. But work is good and should be enjoyable. Our chief motive for working should be to fulfil our purpose. I thoroughly enjoy what I do, as I am proud of what I do, and work is like play to me.

There are volumes of books offering shortcuts to success and financial freedom, but the truth is - there is no true success without hard and smart work.

Thomas Edison, the greatest of inventors, went through hundreds of experiments that were failures before he achieved success with the electric light. He attributed his success to two percent inspiration and ninety-eight percent hard work (perspiration), a formula indeed for incredible accomplishments.

The Principle of Investment

The masses are caught up working for money. We have just finished looking at the Principle of Work. The chief reason why the masses hate work and are bored with their job is because they are only working for a living; they are working for money. It was never God's intention that the primary reason for work was to earn money. We were ordained to good work, so we must work to fulfil our divine purpose.

Investment is money working for us, money must become our slave and it must work for us. So, whilst we are caught up working to fulfil what we were born to do (which of course will bring us money as a benefit) we should have money working for us.

The masses are trapped working for money and regret that they don't have the time and the means to do all they would like to do. Through investment we can get to that place where we have money working for us so that we will be free to work in the areas that we really enjoy.

Investment and re-investment is the key that will break the vicious cycle of just working to merely meet our basic needs, such as paying our bills. If you consume everything that you earn, you are bound to remain in poverty. You must invest, reinvest, and diversify your investment to break the vicious cycle of hand-to-mouth living.

The Principle of Perseverance

The story is told about the American violinist, Fritz Kreister, who at the end of a concert went backstage only to hear a lady say, *"I'd give my life to play as you do!"* He turned and looked at the woman and said, *"Madam, I did."*

The masses do not want to give themselves two or three years, much less a lifetime, to accomplish something, they get discouraged after a few months and give up. But if you are going to succeed you must hang in there and exercise the Principle of Perseverance or what some of my folks would call the good old *"stick-to-it-iveness."* You will meet opposition, criticism, and rejection face to face on your road to success.

Consider the Wright brothers. On the lonely sands to North Carolina's outer banks, they battled the elements, the ridicule of men and the lack of resources. They built, they failed, and they rebuilt and failed again. Finally, they flew and literally changed the world.

You must develop a passion to fulfil your vision so that nothing or nobody should stop you. In the time of trial keep your eyes focused on your vision. Recall Thomas Edison, the greatest of inventors, had such a passion to fulfil his vision that he went through hundreds of experiments that were failures before he achieved success and gave us electric light.

The Principle of Faith

Faith is the victory that causes us to move mountains and accomplish the impossible. Faith generates the power, the know-how and the strength to do what we want to do. When you believe you can do something, the how-to- do-it develops.

Having a dream and believing that the dream can become a reality generates the step it will take to bring that dream to pass. In other words, the how to do it always comes to those who believe they can do it.

Faith generates the power to do. It was faith in the possibility that man could go to the moon that caused it to happen. It was faith that a tunnel under the English Channel to connect England with the continent that made it a reality today.

Faith is the motivating force behind all great books; plays; scientific discoveries; successful businesses; churches; governmental and nongovernmental organizations.

Faith in the negative is called doubt; faith in the positive is called real faith. The story is told of two women who turned seventy years old, yet each focused their faith in two different directions. One said *"My life is coming to an end."*

To her seven decades of living meant that her body must be breaking down and she had better prepare for her grave. The other woman, however, believed that a person is capable of accomplishing what she believes she can do at any age.

Thus, she set a higher standard for herself. She decided that mountain climbing might be a good sport to begin at age seventy. For the next twenty-five years she devoted herself to this new adventure, scaling some of the highest peaks in the world, until today, Hulda Crooks has become the oldest woman to ascend Mount Fuji. Faith is what makes the difference between a joyous, victorious life and one of frustration and misery.

The Principle of Goal setting

Great achievers have an obvious trait in common — goal setting. Writing down their goals is a part of their lifestyle. Goal setting is the step-by-step process towards having your vision turn into reality.

Dr. Myles Munroe says, *"If there is no goal in front of you, you'll check the hazardous holes behind you. If there is no vision in front of you to pull you on, you will be dragged back to the path you know well. If your imagination does not become documented, it will soon ferment into vapor and disillusionment."*

You will never leave where you are right now until you know exactly where you want to be. You must know what you really want before you can obtain it. You will never change your location until you determine your destination! What you see it what you get!

Janice Maxwell tells her story how she became the National Spelling Bee Champion. She put up a banner in her room long before she became the national champion. On that banner she wrote:

JANICE MAXWELL - NATIONAL SPELLING BEE CHAMPION. She was spelling and looking at this banner months before the competition. She had no doubt whatsoever that she was going to win. She saw herself winning — then she worked towards winning.

Someone gave me a sticker once. It said, *"If you can imagine it, you can achieve it. If you can dream it, you can become it."*

Jesus Always Responds to People Who Know What They Want

The woman in Mark 5 knew what she wanted. She had established a goal. She was determined to touch the hem of the garment of Christ. She reached Him and received the miracle she desired.

The fact that God has given you a vision, a clear mental picture of a goal or miracle you want to obtain, is an indication that it exists and is possible. The persistent presence of a God-given desire in the heart is proof that it is possible for you to attain it.

You may be feeling inadequate, inferior, and incapable of achieving your God-given desire, but God gave you your dream for a purpose.

You must realize that faith cannot be released until you have established a clear-cut target and goal.

There are laws and principles that govern this universe. Miracles and blessings do not just happen to us.

One of those Master Keys that will unlock your dream is goal setting. God wants you to focus the desire of your heart and use your faith for its attainment.

I exhort you therefore to establish your goal, discern God's plan for its fulfilment, and launch out in faith towards it.

Great leaders have seldom taken the mantle of leadership for its own sake. True leadership is born out of vision and purpose that is established firmly on the bedrock of conviction and discipline.

Leadership is a means and not the end in itself.

Planning

This is the characteristic, which separates achievers from dreamers. *"He who fails to plan, plans to fail,"* so goes an old proverb.

Planning is both an art and a discipline. Even the greatest artist has to develop his skills; so must the leader develop his ability to plan. Effective planning requires the ability to assimilate and organize facts concerning the realities being dealt with.

Principles and Recommendations Principles:

(1) Despise not the day of small beginning (Zech. 4:10; Job 8:7).
(2) Where God leads, he provides.
(3) Work for purpose and let your money work for you.

(4) Money is bread to eat and seed to sow.

(5) Educate yourself around your gift not away from your gift.

(6) Working for another man's business should be a steppingstone into your own.

Recommendations:

(1) Learn all you can about the business endeavours you plan to get into.

(2) Study basic accounting, management, and marketing.

(3) Those using the Mustard Seed Principle must have -
   a) A clear-cut vision (know where you are going).
   b) Do not try to live off the business immediately; give it 3—5 years to get established.
   c) In the meantime, tithe and sow seed from the profits.
   d) Make sure when you take income from the business you have enough to plough back into it for growth and diversification.
   e) Beware of acquiring things to appear successful, while at the same time hurting the business *(walk before you leap)*.

(4) Diligent hands will rule, but laziness ends in slave labour (Proverbs 12: 24).

All hard work brings profit, but mere talk leads only to poverty (Proverbs 14: 23

Notes

Key Points

_____

_____

_____

_____

_____

_____

Personal Thoughts

_____

_____

_____

_____

Areas for additional research

_____

_____

_____

_____

_____

"They that wait upon the Lord shall renew their strength — They shall mount up with wings as eagles - They shall run and not be weary — they shall walk and not faint" *(Isaiah 40:31).*

This word *'wait'* to some could thus be translated; they that serve the Lord consistently shall renew their strength and mount up with wings as eagles. This is in perfect agreement with Exodus 23: 2526. *"And ye shall serve the Lord your God, and He shall bless thy bread, and thy water, and I will take sickness away from the midst of thee . . . there shall nothing cast their young, nor be barren in thy land; the number of thy days I will fulfill."*

Consistently serving God in the following areas:
(1) Praise/worship
(2) Study and meditation in God's word
(3) Tithing and giving.
(4) Fellowship and communion with other believers
(5) Taking the great commission to the world

Will release four (4) constant promotions in your life.

(1) From faith to faith (Romans 1:16-17)
(2) From glory to glory (II Corinthians 3:18, Proverbs 4:18)

(3) From strength to strength (Psalm 84:3-7)

(4) From wealth to wealth (Psalm 113:14, Genesis 26: 12-14)

Since this book is about economic empowerment, I will be expanding on promotion number four (4) — from wealth to wealth. The scripture says that the Lord shall increase you more and more, both you and your children (Ps 115: 14).

This is a prophetic promise — The Lord shall (not may or might) — increase you more and more. This is exactly what happened to Isaac. Isaac settled in the correct geographical location where God directed him, and he sowed in the land (Gen 26:12).

Within twelve months he reaped an hundredfold. His increase did not stop at the hundredfold; he continued to serve God and as a result the scripture says, *"And the Lord blessed him — and the man waxed great, and went forward, and grew until he became very great"* — one translation says very wealthy, *"for he had possession of flocks, and possession of herds, and great store of servants and the Philistines envied him."*

Isaac was set on the path of no return. He went forward from wealth to wealth. He was operating under the blessing of Abraham. *"Christ hath redeemed us from the curse of the law, being made a curse for us... that the Blessing of Abraham might come on us*" (Galatians 3:14).

What is the blessing of Abraham? The blessing of Abraham states: that we will be the head and not the tail, healthy and not sick, strong, and not weak, rich, and not poor - a success and not a failure.

According to (Deuteronomy 28:1-14) - The blessing of Abraham will overtake us. We will experience the uncommon favour of God - whereby goodness and mercy will be our portion all the days of our lives.

Forget Not All His Benefits

We cannot afford to forget His benefits, notice according to Psalm 103: 2 - it is a warning not to forget them. If you forget a benefit - it will forget you. Have you ever wondered why it is that God said that it is a sure thing that goodness and mercy shall follow us all the days of our lives, yet more than ninety per cent of the body of Christ have more distress following them than goodness and mercy?

They have forgotten God's benefits. Every day I roll out of bed I expect goodness and mercy to follow me. I expect the FOG. Some say, what is the FOG?

FOG is the Favour Of God. I am consciously and anxiously looking for goodness and mercy. Most of God's people it seems arc expecting the devil to follow them around. They even sing the song about Satan is on their track - well too bad for you - Satan is not on my track. For in order for him to get on my track he would have to get saved and there is no salvation for him.

"Therefore, we ought to give the more earnest heed to the things which we have heard, lest at any time we should let them slip." (Hebrews 2:1).

For centuries believers have been allowing the promises of God to slip by, not taking heed to remember and act on them.

God promises that if we delight in the law of the Lord and meditate on it day and night *"We shall be like a tree planted by the rivers of water"* (Psalm 1: 3). Whenever you are reading the word and you come across the word shall, or the phrase shall he watch out! — A sure word of prophecy is coming.

"He shall be like a tree planted by the rivers of water." A tree planted by the rivers of water does not know what it is to have a dry season - yet more than ninety per cent of God's people are always dry and need prayer to overcome their dryness. Ask how many of them are

consistently meditating in God's word day and night, not one - no man dare call God a liar. He said if you meditate on God's word day and night you shall be like a tree planted by the rivers of water and whatsoever you doeth shall prosper.

Whatsoever you doeth shall prosper. Folks who do nothing - even if God prospers nothing a thousand times over you will still end up with nothing.

This reminds me of the story with Nobody - Once they needed a Sunday school teacher. Everybody thought Anybody would do it, and Anybody thought Somebody would do it. And you know who did it? That's exactly right. . . Nobody!

One of the universal laws of God is sowing and reaping. What you sow is what you reap. Invest your time in appropriating, meditating, and acting on God's word and you will reap exactly what He promises.

David said, *"Surely goodness and mercy shall follow me all the days of my life."* The word surely means that it is sure, it is certain. Have you ever wondered why more than ninety per cent of God's people have more distress following them instead of goodness and mercy? The truth is very few are conscientiously and actively looking for God's goodness and mercy. I find that they are more looking for demons and sure enough, those demons are showing up. Most of God's people seem to be more devil focused than God focused.

They are more demon conscious than angel conscious. The more I consciously and anxiously look for God's blessings are the more they are coming my way. So, guess what, I have developed what is called a *"miracle mentality"*.

The scripture says to be carnally minded is death but to be spiritually minded is life and peace. To be carnally minded means to be naturally minded, it's like the portion of scripture, which says *"For the weapons of our warfare are not carnal"* - meaning not natural. So, to be carnally or naturally minded, will produce worry, stress and finally death. Therefore, beloved, it behooves us to be supernaturally, or miracle minded and enjoy life and peace.

The bible says we have the mind of Christ and the spirit of a sound mind. It is a fact that if you tell your mind that something cannot be done - it will get to work and start to manufacture reasons why that something cannot be done. Similarly, tell yourself that something is possible and can be accomplished, and your mind will begin to generate strategies to get what you want done accomplished.

When one considers the awesome feats that have been done, dreams and visions that have been fulfilled by their believing that they could be done, consider how much more can be done by tapping into the mind of Christ. No wonder the Apostle Paul states, *"He is able to do exceedingly, abundantly — above all that we could even ask or think"* (Ephesians 1: 3-19).

Notes

Key Points

_____

_____

_____

_____

_____

Personal Thoughts

_____

_____

_____

Areas for additional research

_____

_____

_____

_____

Seven Benefits the Psalmist David Warns Us Not to Forget in Psalm 103:1-6

(1) Who forgives all our iniquities.
(2) Who healeth all thy diseases.
(3) Who redeemeth thy life from destruction.
(4) Who crowneth thee with loving kindness and tender mercies.
(5) Who satisfieth thy mouth with good things.
(6) Who reneweth thy youth like the eagles.
(7) Who executeth righteousness and judgement on our behalf.

Finally, if you want to stay of the path of no return, the path that shines brighter anti brighter even to the perfect day, the path that moves from one level of faith to the next, the path that causes you to increase in strength and wealth.

Then I leave with you three simple things to do:
(1) Think on God's Word.
(2) Speak God's Word.
(3) Act on God's Word.

About The Author

 Ninety seven percent of the world's population have been socialized to work for money. As such poverty and economic wage slavery continues to a serious problem, especially in the third world.

In "Seven Keys to Economic Empowerment", Dr. Phinn tells you how to reverse this trend so that you can let money work for you, as well as how to earn multiple income.

In 1986 the author used these seven keys which he shared with you, and with a small seed of the Jamaican equivalent of US$150.00 broke the 'backbone' of poverty in his own life.

His Excellency The Right Honorable Dr. Phillip S. Phinn, is an International Christian Ambassador, Apostolic Prophet, Motivational Speaker, Minister, Author, Lecturer, Advisor, Counseling Psychologist, Businessman, Economic and Financial Consultant, teaching mankind how to win the battles of life. He has travelled extensively for over 35 years throughout the Americas and the world as a conference speaker, seminar and convention teacher and lecturer; God confirming his messages with signs and wonders.

In May of 2012, Dr. Phillip S. Phinn was commissioned Commander of the Most Distinguish Order of Extra Ordinary Ambassadors from Word of Life Ministries aka WOLMI. Dr. Phinn is the President General of Word of Life Christian-Fellowship, aka WOLMI, and Chief Ambassador to the United Nations.

Presiding Bishop and Apostolic Prophet of NO Limits Ministries in Brampton Ontario, Canada and of Word of Life Affiliate churches and ministries.

Chaplain/General and Chairman of the Canadian International Chaplaincy Association, also known as Christian International Chaplaincy Association and Chancellor of CICA International University and Seminary.

He is the author of four books and several publications. Dr. Phinn has appeared on several telecasts and spoken on numerous radio shows. He is the Father and Developer of the MUSTARD SEED PRINCIPLE. He has been sharing this principle with thousands around the world and many, who have applied it, have testified to substantial financial breakthroughs.

As a result, he was invited to participate in the first United Nations Global Conference on Sustainable Development for small Island States (SIDS) in Barbados 1994, and the World Summit on Social Development in Copenhagen,-

Denmark, 1995. In November 1996, under his leadership, Word of Life Christian Fellowship was accredited by the United Nations under the follow status: **'NGO in special consultative status with the Economic and Social Council to the United Nations' (ECOSOC).**

Dr. Phinn holds earned doctoral and master's degrees in Theology, Christian Psychology, Leadership and Management from the respective institutions such as- Christian International School of Theology, International Theological Seminary of California, City and Guild Institute of London (UK), Kingdom Covenant Leadership Institute and The Canadian Christian Theological Seminary in Calgary, Alberta Canada.

Currently Dr. Phillip Phinn is married to his beautiful and virtuous wife Sharon J. Baquedo-Phinn. Together they are caring for their three children.

Printed by BoD™in Norderstedt, Germany

9 781312 630031